Royal Tea

By Cindy J. Dlugolecki

A Fairy Tale Play with Music
For the Young

Published by

Blue Moon Plays

For That Once-In-A-Lifetime Blue Moon Experience

Royal Tea © 2012 Cindy J. Dlugolecki
All rights reserved.

Publisher: Blue Moon Plays, LLC
1385 Fordham Road, Ste 105-279
Virginia Beach, VA 23464
Printed in the USA
ISBN # 978-1-943416-92-9

To purchase scripts:

- Purchase sufficient printed hard copies (one for each cast member, plus 3 for the crew) - an automatic 10 percent discount is applied to multiple printed hardcopies at the point of ordering.

Or

- Purchase a Multicopy PDF which allows you to print sufficient copies of this script (one for each cast member, plus 3 for the crew). Click Return to Merchant to download your printable PDF. A link to the download will also be emailed to you, along with a link to the application for performance license.

To apply for a Performance License, go to the Product Page of the play and fill out and submit the application form.

To pay the Performance Fee, simply pay the invoice you will be emailed when we receive your application for performance.

Your Performance License for your requested dates will be emailed to you.

All scripts and licenses shall be obtained at Blue Moon Plays at www.havescripts.com

If you wish to make changes in the script of any kind, you must receive permission from the publisher or the playwright. Permission is usually granted readily when schools or theaters face casting problems and the changes do not affect the quality or intent of the original.

**For information, visit www.havescripts.com;
email info@bluemoonplays.com
or call 757-816-1164**

ROYAL TEA
By Cindy J. Dlugolecki

CAST OF CHARACTERS

WINIFRED--concerned, business-like

LITTLE RED RIDING HOOD--tough sarcastic cookie, ready to be liberated

GOLDILOCKS--Sexy with a vampy Mae West-like inflection; loves attention

AURORA (Sleeping Beauty)—Snores half-way through the play; under a blanket

CINDERELLA--reluctant to give up the good life

RAPUNZEL--gum-popping valley girl

FAIRY GODMOTHER

COSTUMES: Princess characters should all have wigs, crowns/tiaras and be elegantly dressed. Only Rapunzel should have short hair, covered with a ski cap and her tiara. Little Red Riding Hood is all in red and has a picnic basket at her feet.

SET: Two card tables set with tablecloths, water glasses, coffee cups, and ice cream dishes. Three women sit at each table.

NOTE FROM PLAYWRIGHT: Although it looks like this play is written for women only, at a preliminary reading a man took the role of Aurora. Casting some men as fairytale women would create additional humor.

(AURORA sleeps under a blanket on a chair at a table. WINIFRED, GOLDILOCKS, LITTLE RED RIDING HOOD, CINDERELLA, and RAPUNZEL enter the stage one by one singing the line, "Once upon a time.")

ONCE UPON A TIME
ONCE UPON A TIME
ONCE UPON A TIME
ONCE UPON A TIME
ONCE UPON A TIME
ONCE UPON A TIME
  (Together)
ONCE UPON A TIME
ONCE UPON A TIME

ONCE UPON A TIME
IS HOW THE STORY STARTS
WITH A TALE OF LOVE AND LOSS
TO STILL AND THRILL YOUR HEARTS.
ONCE UPON A TIME
IN A WOODED FOREIGN LAND
THERE'S A KING AND QUEEN WHO THINK
THEIR DAUGHTER NEEDS A MAN!

    WINIFRED, RAPUNZEL
FROTHY, FLOWING GOWNS
TIARAS AND OUR PEARLS

  CINDERELLA, LITTLE RED RIDING HOOD, GOLDILOCKS
THOUGH SOME OF US ARE VERY PLAIN
JUST COMMON LITTLE GIRLS.

    ALL WITH BLONDE HAIR
BLONDE HEADS WITHOUT A BRAIN
IS HOW WE'RE LOOKED UPON.

ALL

HOW WILL WE SURVIVE THIS WORLD
WITHOUT A MAN OF BRAWN?

WITCHES AND WOLVES
DRAGONS AND DEATH
DRAGONS AND WOLVES
WITH REALLY BAD BREATH.
AND THEN BY MAGIC
A STRONG MAN ARRIVES
YES TO SAVE THE DAY

(A tall, handsome, charming, well-dressed, strong man with good teeth on a big white horse arrives.)

CINDERELLA

HE PROMISED ME LOVE

WINIFRED

HE PROMISED ME BLISS

ALL

MYSTERY AND MAGIC
IN HIS TOUCH AND IN HIS KISS
HAPP'LY EVER AFTER
IS HOW THE STORY ENDS
WHEN WE SAID "I DO" IN FRONT
OF FAMILY AND FRIENDS.

(Sung as WOMEN gather by the tables for tea)

ALL

ONCE UPON A TIME
ONCE UPON A TIME
WE ALL LIVED HAPP'LY EVER AFTER
ONCE UPON A TIME.

WINIFRED
(Tapping a knife on her water glass)
Ladies, ladies, we all have busy lives . . . manicures . . .
pedicures . . . shopping—-

GOLDILOCKS
Don't forget massages. I have a handsome, young
masseuse. Some massage too hard. Some massage too
light. He massages my delicate muscles just right.

LITTLE RED RIDING HOOD
(Sarcastically)
Oooo. He massages my delicate muscles just right.

GOLDILOCKS
(Glaring at Little Red Riding Hood, then Winfred)
My appointment's at two!

WINIFRED
Ladies, ladies. Time spent here means less time in the
hot tub, by the castle pool . . . or in Goldilocks' case, with
her "just right" masseuse. If everyone has finished her
tea and fat-free yogurt, I hereby call this support group
of fairy tale women to order.
(Looking about)
Snow White missed our entire luncheon, and that's not
like her. Does anyone know where she is?

GOLDILOCKS

Snow White would be crazy to show up to have lunch with all of us. (*Sexily*) I hear she's enjoying the company of SEVEN men.

LITTLE RED RIDING HOOD

CLEANING UP after seven men is more like it. Snow White puts the toilet seat down more times in one day than all of you lay down your credit cards!

GOLDILOCKS
(*Ignoring her comment*)
Seven men, imagine! And I had to live with three bears. I'd trade places with Snow White any day!

(*AURORA snores loudly. ALL but WINIFRED giggle and shake their heads*)

WINIFRED
(*Tapping on her glass*)
Order. Order. May I continue? Thank you.
(*To everyone gathered*)
My fairy tale friends, I know you're wondering why I invited everyone here today. The truth is . . . I've read some bad news in the *Fairy Tale Times*.

RAPUNZEL

Like . . . the what?

WINIFRED

The Fairy Tale Times? Your don't read it, Rapunzel? You must. All of you. It's imperative to keep up on current events.

LITTLE RED RIDING HOOD
Or sales on frozen peas, huh, Winifred?

CINDERELLA
Not funny, Little Red.

GOLDILOCKS
Some people read the paper for serious current events.
Some people read the paper for funny comics. I read the
paper for personal ads . . . for my personal needs, if you
know what I mean. I find that just right.

LITTLE RED RIDING HOOD
Did you hear that? Goldilocks reads! That's headline
news in and of itself. I would think some words would be
too hard. Some words would be too easy. Nice to know
some words are just right!

CINDERELLA
Testy today, aren't we, Little Red Riding Hood? Here,
you need something to sweeten your disposition.

*(CINDERELLA sprinkles a sugar packet on LRR.
AURORA snores loudly.)*

WINIFRED
(Tapping glass)
Ladies, ladies. *(Clearing throat)* May I continue? I have
very bad news, remember?
(beat, taking a deep breath)
Our Fairy Godmother—

CINDERELLA
--has died

                    WINIFRED
NO!

                    GOLDILOCKS
Was she eaten by a bear?

                    WINIFRED
NO!

            LITTLE RED RIDING HOOD
It was wolf!

                    WINIFRED
NO!

                    CINDERELLA
It was a poisoned apple, wasn't it? Snow White knows all
about those.

                    WINIFRED
ABSOLUTELY NOT!
          (*beat, calming everyone, taking a breath*)
Our fairy godmother . . . is retiring.

          (*There are sighs of shock. AURORA snores.*)

            LITTLE RED RIDING HOOD
Wait a minute.
          (*with a disgusted face gesturing to Sleeping
          Beauty*)
Retiring like our own Sleeping Beauty here . . . or retiring
like "Sayonaro, I'm outta here!"

WINIFRED

Our beloved Fairy Godmother is getting older. She's tired. Says it's time for a change. She just can't drop everything and come to our rescue whenever we need her anymore. Especially if she's in the middle of her Zumba class.

LITTLE RED RIDING HOOD

Rather selfish of the F-G, don't you think? Not that I need her. In fact I'm better off without her.

CINDERELLA

Without our Fairy Godmother?
> (*opening another sugar packet and sprinkling it*)

How can you be so sour?

LITTLE RED RIDING HOOD

Just as I was ready to karate chop the Big Bad Wolf in MY story, in comes a big, strong, hunk of a man to get the glory instead of me. The F-G sent him. Like I couldn't handle the wolf myself. Makes me bitter. I for one think it's time for the F-G to go!

(AURORA snores.)

WINIFRED

Now, now. Little Red, we should get better, not bitter. We have lots of little girls to inspire.

LITTLE RED RIDING HOOD

When did you turn into Dr. Phil?

CINDERELLA

Whatever will we do without Fairy Godmother's magic?

RAPUNZEL

She can't retire. Like, hasn't she heard the word "vacation" already. Take a break and come back. Some of us, like, still need her help.
(Pulling off her cap)
Just look at my hair!

GOLDILOCKS
(Breathlessly & sexy)
Aurora's hair is too long. Rapunzel's hair is too short. (Smugly) Thank goodness some of us in fairytale land have hair that is just right.

LITTLE RED RIDING HOOD
(Mocking)
Thank goodness some of us in fairytale land have hair that is just right.

(LRR puts finger in mouth to gag. AURORA snores.)

WINIFRED
Order! Ladies, I called this meeting to discuss the ramifications of Fairy Godmother's retirement. We have to be realistic. And Cinderella raised a very good question. What do we do without Fairy Godmother's magic?

CINDERELLA
Where will I get my clothes? Fairy Godmother would wave her wand and presto, I had a new gown, with matching accessories. I didn't have to worry about jewelry or tiaras. Thank goodness I still have glass slippers that go with EVERYTHING!

LITTLE RED RIDING HOOD
(Mocking)
Thank goodness I have glass slippers that go with
everything! HELLO! Cinderella, there ARE more
important issues than how to accessorize!

WINIFRED
(Sternly)
Ladies! (Regaining composure) What I am about to say
will no doubt be unpopular. But I have given her
retirement a great deal of thought and . . . I have come to
a startling revelation. I think we all lead rather self-
centered lives.

(There are gasps of astonishment from all but
LITTLE RED RIDING HOOD, who stands and
applauds.)

LITTLE RED RIDING HOOD
(Standing and applauding)
Finally! Someone admits the shallowness of many fairy
tale women and the absurdity of some of the stories. Will
this be on You-Tube, 'cause I want proof!

WINIFRED
(Giving LRRH a nod, continuing)
I for one am rather tired thinking only of what to wear at
the next royal ball or planning the menu for some
elegant state dinner.

(ALL but LITTLE RED RIDING HOOD buzz in
disagreement.)

LITTLE RED RIDING HOOD
You Go, Girl!

RAPUNZEL
So, like, what are you proposing, Princess Winifred?

WINIFRED
(Swallowing)
I propose we go to college . . . learn a skill . . . get a job . .
. pursue a career.

(There are collective gasps of horror.)

RAPUNZEL
(Squeaking, horrified)
Like, work?!

WINIFRED
We could make over the world!

CINDERELLA
No, no, no. I've been down that road. I've cleaned
fireplaces, scoured toilets, and scrubbed floors. I like the
life I have. Oh, why did Fairy Godmother retire?

RAPUNZEL
Like, did she say "makeover?"

GOLDILOCKS
Some jobs would be too hard. Some jobs would be too
easy. How will I ever find a job just right . . . for me?

(AURORA snores.)

LITTLE RED RIDING HOOD
Winifred, I'm proud of you. No one has ever dared to
challenge the majestic role! I want to hear more!

RAPUNZEL
Didn't I, like, hear "make-over?"

LITTLE RED RIDING HOOD
Leave it to Rapunzel to segue from making over the
world to making over her face!

WINIFRED
Now. Now. Don't be cruel to poor Rapunzel. None of us
would take kindly to some wicked witch cutting off our
hair. Talk about bad hair days!

LITTLE RED RIDING HOOD
But I'm tired of her whining all the time. (To Rapunzel)
Rapunzel, wake up and smell the hairspray. Stop
wallowing in something that will grow back and grow up!

(AURORA snores.)

WINIFRED
I know we can do it, Ladies. All of us, including you,
Rapunzel. We have the intelligence . . . we have the
finesse . . . we have the estrogen! It's time we fairy tale
females take a stand, never again waiting to be rescued
or led about by a man, no matter how charming!

CINDERELLA
What! *(Faltering)* No Prince Charmings?

LITTLE RED RIDING HOOD
(Delighted)
No men?

GOLDILOCKS
Some men are too hot. Some men are too cold.
(Seductively)
But some men are just right.

(Sound of a DRAGON roaring very loudly offstage)

AURORA
(Suddenly wakes up, wide-eyed and wondering)
What . . . was that?

RAPUNZEL
Look! Like the chandeliers are shaking!

CINDERELLA
Is it a dragon? It's a dragon! What do we do? My Prince
Charming's at the gym and Fairy Godmother has retired.
Oh woe is me!

RAPUNZEL
Like, woe is US!

AURORA
Coffee's spilling all over the tablecloth. And I need that
caffeine!

RAPUNZEL
If it's a dragon . . . a fire-breathing dragon . . . it will burn
off any hair I have left Like, help!!!

CINDERELLA
(Wailing)
Where is Fairy Godmother when we need her?

LITTLE RED RIDING HOOD
(Picking up a chair to use as a weapon)
Stifle, Cindy. I LOVE it. Bring it on, Dragon! I'm not scared.

GOLDILOCKS
(Putting her hands up to her face in mock horror)
Ooo. Ooo. That growl is too loud to be a dog. That growl is too soft to be a bear. But it sounds just right for an angry dragon.

AURORA
Can I get some coffee?

(DRAGON roars and AURORA hides under table.)

GOLDILOCKS
And I bet he's big. Bigger than little baby bear, bigger than the middle-sized mama bear, bigger than the biggest papa bear! BIG! Who's going to rescue us now? I still want to get my massage at four o'clock.

AURORA
(Holding her cup out from the table, awaiting service)
Yoo hoo. Coffee.

LITTLE RED RIDING HOOD
Oh, Goldilocks . . . you make me sick! Too big, too little . . . too fat, too thin . . . too hot, too cold. Cut the English

lesson on antonyms and get a life. I for one am sick of being rescued by big strong men.

WINIFRED
It's time for all of us to inform all the big bad wolves and the fire-breathing dragons in the world that we can take care of ourselves!

AURORA
Not without coffee. I need caffeine.

(DRAGON roars again offstage.)

RAPUNZEL
Oh, dear. The dragon must have, like, heard that Fairy Godmother retired.

AURORA
(Shocked, tentatively sitting back in her chair)
She retired?

RAPUNZEL
So like, what are we going to do about the dragon?

AURORA
Fairy Godmother retired? Why am I always the last to know?

CINDERELLA
Oh, dear. We have no pumpkins or mice or magic to make an escape! What are we going to do?

LITTLE RED RIDING HOOD
Try throwing sugar packets on it, Cindy. Maybe they're magic. Though they didn't make me any sweeter.

AURORA

Caffeine's all the magic I need. I feel like I've been asleep for a hundred years.

LITTLE RED RIDING HOOD
(Putting hands on hips, emphatically)
DUH!

(DRAGON roars really loudly.)

GOLDILOCKS
Oh, oh, oh. The dragon sounds like he's right outside!

WINIFRED
(Boldly)
Ladies, our time has come to prove ourselves. I'm going to invite the dragon in.

LITTLE RED RIDING HOOD
Hallelujah. I'll get the door!

GOLDILOCKS
No! What if it's a fire-breathing dragon who will sizzle the castle in flames like the burgers at Burgers 'R' Us? Some of us will be well done, some of us will be rare . . . oh but others of us will be just right!

RAPUNZEL
What if, like, he's a hungry dragon who will voraciously gobble us up like jujubes at a Sunday matinee?

LITTLE RED RIDING HOOD
Well then, Rapunzel, you wouldn't have to worry about your hair anymore!

AURORA

Jujubes. Someone has jujubes. If I can't have caffeine, candy will work.

GOLDILOCKS

What if it's a spiteful dragon that would swirl the castle and us into the air like matchsticks in a tornado and--

FAIRY GODMOTHER (O.S. in deep male voice)

Enough already. I'm not getting any younger!

*(LRR opens the door. FAIRY GODMOTHER enters .
. . ALL the women gasp.)*

ALL WOMEN TOGETHER

Fairy Godmother?

FAIRY GODMOTHER

What? I'm retired. Not dead!

LITTLE RED RIDING HOOD

I gotta admire your style, F-G!

FAIRY GODMOTHER

Thanks, I think, Red.

RAPUNZEL

Did you, like, see a dragon outside? Like, we were expecting a dragon.

AURORA

How did you get past the dragon that so rudely interrupted my nap?

CINDERELLA
She must have used her magic! Oh, thank goodness.
You're still using magic. The newspaper lied! You're not
retiring.

FAIRY GODMOTHER
Yes, I am. I used the dragon voice to get your attention.
Evidently it worked. I wanted one last moment with you
before I left. Time to be frank.

RAPUNZEL
Didn't you just say, like, you were Fairy Godmother?

FAIRY GODMOTHER
(To *audience, rolling her eyes*)
Is it any wonder I need a break?

(To WOMEN, singing TWEET ME ON TWITTER)

I'VE KNOWN YOU ALL FOREVER
THROUGH THICK AND THIN, YOU UNDERSTAND
TOO BAD THAT THROUGH THE YEARS
YOU'RE THINNER. I'M THICKER. OH MAN.
THERE'S SO MUCH LOVE INSIDE MY HEART
IT'S NOW HARD FOR ME TO SAY
TO MY B-F-FS GATHERED HERE
THIS F-G IS GOING AWAY!

CHORUS
FIND ME ON FACEBOOK.
TWEET ME ON TWITTER
I HAVE RETIRED
PLEASE DON'T BE BITTER

DO STAY IN TOUCH SO
FRIENDSHIPS DON'T WITHER
FIND ME ON FACEBOOK
TWEET ME ON TWITTER.

WITH A SPRINKLE OF FAIRY DUST,
FLICKS OF THE WAND IN MY HAND
SUMMONING WITH SECRET SPELLS
A SAVIOR, A HERO, A MAN!
PERHAPS I DID NOT SERVE YOU WELL
TO SAVE YOU FROM YOUR WOES
INSTEAD OF A MAN YOU NEEDED PLANS
TO BE A FEMALE DYNAMO!

BRIDGE
FOLKS ASK THIS FAIRY
IF I WANT TO MARRY
I SAY NOT ON YOUR LIFE
I'M SINGLE AND FREE
FREE TO BE ME
I AM NOBODY'S WIFE!

CHORUS
FIND ME ON FACEBOOK.
TWEET ME ON TWITTER
I HAVE RETIRED
PLEASE DON'T BE BITTER
DO STAY IN TOUCH SO
FRIENDSHIPS DON'T WITHER
FIND ME ON FACEBOOK
TWEET ME ON TWITTER.

FINAL CHORUS
VIEW ME ON YOU-TUBE
GOOGLE AND HULU

E-MAIL, TEXT, CALL ME
READ MY BLOG AND SEE
I'M NOT A SITTER
I'M GONNA FLITTER
BYE BYE STORYBOOKS
FORGET THE PHONEBOOK
FIND ME ON FACEBOOK
TWEET ME ON TWITTER.

FAIRY GODMOTHER
Look, ladies, I have to get to the airport. Catching the first flight available to Tahiti, the south of France, or Disneyworld. I need some space, warm weather, and to ride those teacups everyone talks about. Besides, I finally figured out I'm not really helping you by always being there to wave my magic wand and make things better. It's time for all of you to rely on your own ingenuity and fend for yourselves.

GOLDILOCKS
(Sexil)y
I think I already fend very well for myself, thank you very much.

LITTLE RED RIDING HOOD
She means OUTSIDE the bedroom, Blondie!

GOLDILOCKS
You mean . . . oh don't tell me . . . we may have to learn to "cook"?

(EVERYONE gasps.)

FAIRY GODMOTHER
Either that or use your own cell phone to order take-out.

WINIFRED

I'm ready to cook every fresh and frozen pea in the land!

RAPUNZEL

With all due respect, Fairy Godmother, it's like none of us will ever be blonde enough . . .

GOLDILOCKS

Some of us are.

CINDERELLA

Classy enough . . .

GOLDILOCKS

Some of us are.

AURORA

Or rested enough!

GOLDILOCKS

Some of us are.

CINDERELLA

How will we ever keep our Prince Charmings without your magic to keep us thin, blond, and fashionably dressed? Our lives, as we know it, are over!

FAIRY GODMOTHER

Nonsense! Welcome to the real world. If you ever leave fairytale land, you'll discover that life doesn't necessarily have a happy ending.

AURORA

So, there's no happily ever after?

FAIRY GODMOTHER
Girlfriend, your prince charming snores. That's why I let you sleep for 100 years. You'll never ever have a good night's rest again. Ladies, I'm here today to make you think. Tell me, does being a fairytale princess really make you happy?

WINIFRED
I've never wanted to confess this . . . but . . . I for one have to jump through too many hoops and sleep on too many mattresses to please my royal mother-in-law! And I'm still black and blue and bruised. What a royal pain in the butt!

CINDERELLA
I know I'll never be good enough for my mother-in-law. She looks at me and snickers every time we have pumpkin pie. And if that's not enough . . .
    (sniffling)
my prince charming spends too much time with the young and pretty castle interns!

LITTLE RED RIDING HOOD
Ah-ha! Just as I suspected. Some prince charmings are not so charming!!!!

FAIRY GODMOTHER
And sadly, in real life, there's no fairy Godmother to wave a magic wand to make them disappear. Sometimes Prince Charmings are really MONSTERS in disguise.

LITTLE RED RIDING HOOD
Yeah. I want all you to know that I hate Valentine's Day. It's the only day I wear black!

RAPUNZEL

Like I so don't want to hear this. My Prince Charming's wonderful. Like, he loves me! He really loves me.

FAIRY GODMOTHER

Tell me something, Rapunzel. Are you ready to put all your dreams on hold to please your prince?

RAPUNZEL
(swooning)
Like, yes. I LOVE him!

FAIRY GODMOTHER

And you're willing to polish his armor . . . sort his socks . . . and keep his castle clean till death do you part from your laundry detergent, vacuum cleaner, and silver polish?

RAPUNZEL

Like, yes. I'll do anything for him.

FAIRY GODMOTHER

And you're willing to bear his children, change diapers, and wipe runny noses while you are still a child yourself . . . when you really don't know who you are and what your gifts are?

RAPUNZEL

So like anything for love! Anything for my Prince Charming . . . so handsome . . . so brave . . .

LITTLE RED RIDING HOOD
(To audience)
So disgusting!

FAIRY GODMOTHER
(Waving hands and shaking head emphatically)
NONONONONONO. Listen, chickiepoos, all of you.
Family life and marriage can be wonderful with the right
person . . . but I should have made you wait until you're
older. I'm sorry for promoting the fairy tale hoopla about
"handsome" Prince Charmings and happily ever afters.
    (beat)
What if Prince Charming NEVER arrives on the scene?
That happens in real life. And a "charming" man doesn't
guarantee a "good" man. Unfortunately, I helped the
Brothers Grimm promote that myth and the myth that
every woman needs a man to rescue her. I've had
enough . . . and so should you.
    (beat)
You want a happy ending? Find out who YOU are . . . and
then wait for the man who TRULY cares about you . . .
what

FAIRY GODMOTHER
you think . . . and who you want to be. He should
appreciate you as you are. Now, HE would be charming.
Meanwhile, you learn to take care of yourself, and that
starts with being physically fit. Like me, I finally joined a
gym.

ALL but LRR
Gym?

AURORA
You mean with treadmills?

CINDERELLA
Weight machines?

RAPUNZEL
Spinning classes?

GOLDILOCKS
You mean we have to (*beat*) sweat?

FAIRY GODMOTHER
I'm afraid so.

LITTLE RED RIDING HOOD
YES!

CINDERELLA
So where do we go from here? Without our Prince
Charmings. Without you. Without your magic!

FAIRY GODMOTHER
Oh, but Honey, there is magic.

RAPUNZEL
What? Again, like, is anyone else confused?

FAIRY GODMOTHER
Look inside yourselves. I'm not the only one with magic.
You have magic too! And I apologize for keeping you
from finding your own magic before today. Especially to
you, Little Red Riding Hood.

LITTLE RED RIDING HOOD
(Giving her a hug, wailing)
This is the best day of my life!

CINDERELLA
Looks like the sugar finally kicked in!

AURORA
I could still use some coffee.

WINIFRED
There's time for coffee later, Aurora. Isn't this what I've been trying to tell all of you? We can go to college. Become professors, doctors, astronauts, even politicians.

ALL
Politicians? Why?

WINIFRED
To change the rules . . . then rule the changes. We can do it!

FAIRY GODMOTHER
GLORY HALLELUJAH! Isn't the Statue of Liberty a woman! Now I know it won't be easy. And I suspect, that before you face the world for the first time without your Fairy Godmother you may need something to give you confidence . . . an emotional boost.

RAPUNZEL
Like, a makeover?

GOLDILOCKS
Peroxide?

CINDERELLA
A credit card?

WINIFRED
How about a voter registration card?

AURORA
Cappuccino?

LITTLE RED RIDING HOOD
A restraining order!

FAIRY GODMOTHER
Now, Little Red Riding Hood, we don't want to alienate men altogether.

GOLDILOCKS
(Boisterously)
Amen! (More subdued) Amen.

FAIRY GODMOTHER
No, all of you need a theme song!

ALL TOGETHER
A theme song?

AURORA
But I'm hungry for coffee and dessert.

FAIRY GODMOTHER
This is your dessert, Aurora. Your just desserts. Everybody, up. I'll lead.

(THEY all rise, looking a little unsure.)

RAPUNZEL
Fairy Godmother?

FAIRY GODMOTHER
Yes, Rapunzel.

RAPUNZEL
Like, does this mean I now have to pump my own gas?

FAIRY GODMOTHER
We'll talk. Altogether now. Come on, Ladies. Belt it out.
With feeling!

ALL

VERSE 1
GOODBYE BROTHERS GRIMM
LISTEN TO OUR HYMN
WE SING IN CELEBRATION
OF OUR NEW-FOUND INDEPENDENCE
GOODBYE BROTHERS GRIMM
THIS IS NOT A WHIM
WE DEMAND EMANCIPATION
FROM YOUR CONDESCENDENCE.

CHORUS
OUR MAGIC DOESN'T END AT MIDNIGHT
FORGET SPELLS AND WISHING WELLS
WHO NEEDS PRINCES, SHINING KNIGHTS
TO SAVE THE DAY AND EVIL SMITE.
ALL WE NEED IS RIGHT INSIDE
WHERE LAUGHTER, LOVE AND LIGHT RESIDE
NO WANDS WAVING FAIRY DUST
THE MAGIC'S INSIDE US!

VERSE 2
GOODBYE BROTHERS GRIMM
WE'LL TAKE IT FROM HERE
WE'RE ENDING NOT DEFENDING
THE MESSAGE THAT YOU'RE SENDING
GOODBYE BROTHERS GRIMM
WE'VE NOTHING TO FEAR
WE WILL FIGHT SO WE CAN WRITE
OUR STORY'S HAPPY ENDING

CHORUS
OUR MAGIC DOESN'T END AT MIDNIGHT
FORGET SPELLS AND WISHING WELLS
WHO NEEDS PRINCES, SHINING KNIGHTS
TO SAVE THE DAY AND EVIL SMITE.
ALL WE NEED IS RIGHT INSIDE
WHERE LAUGHTER, LOVE AND LIGHT RESIDE
NO WANDS WAVING FAIRY DUST
THE MAGIC'S INSIDE US!

VERSE 3
GOODBYE BROTHERS GRIMM
THERE'S MAGIC WITHIN
NO MORE HAPP'LY EVER AFTER
ALL BECAUSE SOME MEN DARE AND DO
GOODBYE BROTHERS GRIMM
GOODBYE TO YOUR SPIN
HELLO TO ME AND YOU AND YOU AND YOU
OH HALLELU!

CHORUS
OUR MAGIC DOESN'T END AT MIDNIGHT
FORGET SPELLS AND WISHING WELLS
WHO NEEDS PRINCES, SHINING KNIGHTS
TO SAVE THE DAY AND EVIL SMITE.

ALL WE NEED IS RIGHT INSIDE
WHERE LAUGHTER, LOVE AND LIGHT RESIDE
NO WANDS WAVING FAIRY DUST
THE MAGIC'S INSIDE US!

THE END

www.ingramcontent.com/pod-product-compliance
Lightning Source LLC
LaVergne TN
LVHW051713080426
835511LV00017B/2894